Round the Corner and Away We Go

by David J. Gonzol

SMC 567

SCHOTT

Mainz • London • Madrid • New York • Paris • Prague • Tokyo • Toronto

Illustration: *Das tanzende Bauernpaar*
(The Dancing Peasant Couple)
by Albrecht Dürer, 1514

SMC 567

ISMN   M-60001-041-7
UPC   841886004078
ISBN   1-902455-43-6

Design, typesetting and music engraving by William Holab

Contents

Introduction 1

Instrumentarium and Instrument Abbreviations 3

Lucy Locket 4

Down Came a Lady 6

Alabama Gal 8

Lead through That Sugar and Tea 10

Here We Go Zootie-O 12

Li'l 'Liza Jane 14

Stooping on the Window 16

Hanging out the Linen Clothes 20

Follow the Drinking Gourd 22

Round the Corner, Sally 24

Who Killed Cock Robin? 26

Down in That Valley 30

Cedar Swamp 32

INTRODUCTION

This folk song collection provides models of arrangements to be taught using Orff Schulwerk processes. One might ask, how can learning yet another arrangement be valuable? Is it in any way creative? Why do Orff Schulwerk teachers teach ready-made arrangements? An even larger question is: why use accompaniments with folk songs that were originally unaccompanied? Games such as *Lucy Locket*, for example, have been played countless times with great gusto and no instruments. Why would it need an accompaniment? Three reasons come to mind.

First, the strength of teaching Orff Schulwerk arrangements is that it builds the music gradually in the minds and bodies of the students so that their mental and physical understanding grows surely and thoroughly—much in the way composers or arrangers work. It helps students experience an authentic creative process.

Second, folk repertoire can lend itself to a thickening of texture that supports and enhances. In contemporary North America we sing folk songs so extraordinarily seldom in comparison to previous eras, and when we do it tends to be with accompaniment. Historically, people have gathered socially to improvise accompaniments, or composers have published their own arrangements, as Beethoven did with his settings of Irish folk songs. Why is this? The answer seems to lie in how accompaniments complement a song. A steady xylophone heightens the chase in *Lucy Locket* and a doleful recorder increases the mournfulness in *Who Killed Cock Robin?* Adding a complementary part can in itself teach more about a song.

The third reason is that arrangements can be models. Kentucky songs sound like other Kentucky songs because they themselves serve Kentuckians as models. Bach looked to the concertos of Vivaldi. We wish to teach students to be not only melodically creative but also texturally and polyphonically creative. We may teach students an arrangement from the original *Music for Children* volumes but include the students' own alterations and adaptations to give them creative practice. There is also much value in teaching an arrangement unaltered, as long as it serves the musical purpose of teaching some musical concept that can later be transferred for use in another context.

The following arrangements may be taught as printed or used as the basis for creative extensions—or both. In singing *Lucy Locket* monophonically, students learn much about a *mi-sol-la* song for children, a type American Orff Schulwerk teachers treasure. In trying a steady beat drone on the xylophone, students find that it complements the song because it is different from the melody, yet it supports the song. This same technique can be applied to other songs. In experimenting with ostinati, students find that certain patterns are more complementary than others.

The *Lucy Locket* arrangement then is somewhat flexible in that it can be altered but also, hopefully, because it is a useful model as printed. Other arrangements may be less flexible but they still serve as Orff Schulwerk models—if indeed the careful teacher goes on to extend what was learned from the arrangement. That extension might come in another very different lesson. For example, it might come in performing the arrangement of *Alabama Gal* as the A-section of a rondo, alternating with improvisatory sections.

Teaching these arrangements can be highly creative. This book illustrates many of the basic practices used by Orff Schulwerk teachers. Examples of some techniques are:

- teach students to sing the song first
- teach them to perform the bass part, but as body percussion (e.g., patsching it on the thighs)
- transfer the body percussion to the actual bass instrument(s)
- teach students another part, often an inner voice, as body percussion (stamping, patsching, clapping, or snapping)
- transfer that to the instrument
- continue in the same way with other parts; frequently, a "color" part—likely the glockenspiel part, often the sparest—is saved for last.

The songs in this collection can be taught by rote. Teaching them through echoing one phrase at a time can be effective. However, if students are proficient at reading music, that is possible, too. Similar gradual processes can be applied in teaching instrumental parts as well. Moreover, it is often effective to demonstrate an instrumental part in a simplified version, then to add in gradually, one at a time, each complexity until the full version is learned. This volume includes examples of this type of process teaching.

The heart of Orff Schulwerk teaching involves a healthy balance between taking from what exists and making something new. When using good models, valuable lessons about songs and accompaniments can be learned. With creativity, students learn to think or do independently.

Take these songs and arrangements, then, and teach them as written or adapt them as you wish. Yet, teach them always with student creativity in mind. If the arrangement allows, adapt and alter. If it is feasible, include improvisation, or use it as a springboard for a different project. This is what makes teaching Orff Schulwerk highly creative for the instructors, as they fit these lessons into their curricula. I present these arrangements with the hope that they will serve such purposes well.

—David J. Gonzol

INSTRUMENTARIUM AND INSTRUMENT ABBREVIATIONS

V	Voice
SR	Soprano Recorder
AR	Alto Recorder
SG	Soprano Glockenspiel
AG	Alto Glockenspiel
SX	Soprano Xylophone
AX	Alto Xylophone
SM	Soprano Metallophone
AM	Alto Metallophone
Tri.	Triangle
HC	Hanging Cymbal
WB	Wood Block
Gui.	Guiro
HD	Hand Drum
SD	Snare Drum
Bon.	Bongo
Tamb.	Tambourine
Con.	Conga
BD	Bass Drum
BX	Bass Xylophone
BM	Bass Metallophone
CBB	Contrabass Bars

LUCY LOCKET

Concepts:

mi   sol   la

Teaching Suggestions:

- Clapping the beat can be transformed into the hand drum pattern, which is composed of the only two rhythms in the song itself: ♩ and ♫. Both this pattern and the beat can be clapped while playing.
- After the bass xylophone and hand drum parts are transferred to instruments, the triangle part can be taught by modeling.
- An introduction may be invented.

Game:

Lucy Locket is played like *Duck, Duck, Goose*, sitting in a circle—but with this fine folk tune. One child skips around the outside, on the last note dropping a "pocket" (or "wallet") in back of someone. That someone gives chase. If the skipping child arrives back at the chaser's spot first, the chaser must skip next. Otherwise, the first child must try again. Home rules can be made up as needed with regard to the chasing direction (both ways or one?), whether the wallet must be picked up or not, etc.

Lucy Locket

arranged by David J. Gonzol

Exuberantly

Voice: Lu - cy Lock - et lost her pock - et, Kit - ty Fish - er found it.

Triangle

Hand Drum

Bass Xylophone

V: Not a pen - ny was there in it, on - ly rib - bon round it.

Tri.

HD

BX

DOWN CAME A LADY

Concepts:

sol   la   do   mi

Down Came a Lady can provide opportunities for exploration with numbers, colors, rhymes, and drama. A few colored scarves and simple invitations to rhyme ("Down came a lady, down came three . . .") can get students started. Who is Lord Dan'el? Can the ladies be named? Why are they coming down, and what is their story?

Teaching Suggestions:

- Ask the students what kind of rhythm is used on the words "two" and "blue"— a half note—one may say *too* (or rhythm syllable of choice). Ask what rhythm is used for "Down came a" (♩ ♫). Repeat ♩ ♩ ♫ four times for the tambourine ostinato.

  For the bass xylophone part, first play with the left hand only the three Es:

  Then add the B with the right hand:

Help the students discover that the bass xylophone rhythm is the tambourine rhythm backwards, and that both include a half note.

- Construct the recorder part entirely out of half notes, two of them tied.
- Ask: The soprano glockenspiel rhythm is ♩ ♫ ♩ ♩ one time and ♩ ♩ ♩ the other, but where during the song does each of these patterns occur? In experimenting, students can learn that the glockenspiel rhythms complement, rather than duplicate, rhythms of the melody.
- Shall the texture change for new verses?
- Is an introduction needed?

Down Came a Lady

Virginia Folk Song
arranged by David J. Gonzol

ALABAMA GAL

Concepts:

sol la do re mi sol

Teaching Suggestions:

- The song is helpful for teaching syncopation.
- The bass xylophone part can be learned through patsching and the suggested rhythmic speech.
- In teaching the more challenging alto xylophone part, remove the B and F bars. The first measure can be simplified by playing all of the right hand pitches only:

 Repeat three times.

- The left hand note A can be added in,

followed one at a time adding A D D, also with the left hand:

   The fourth measure can be taught with speech, perhaps saving the final word "how" for last of all.
- Snaps and speech can be used to teach the alto glockenspiel part.
- Clapping and speech can be used to learn the hand drum part.
- Experiment alternating full accompaniment with partial textures or improvised solos.

Dance:

Verse 1: Contra dance formation (two facing lines). The head couple sashays to the foot and back.

   Verses 2–4: The head couple reels to the foot: The head boy and second girl reach for each other's right hand; the head girl and second boy do likewise (the head couple passes right shoulders). They each do a half turn. Back together, the head couple joins left hands and does a half turn. The head couple moves on to the third couple offering right hands, turning half way around, then they do another left hand turn together and continue in this manner until they have turned all couples and reached the foot. Verses 2–4 may be repeated until the head couple is safely at the foot, or, before they get there, a new head couple may start reeling with verse 1 (be careful of collisions!). Elbow swings may be used—just enough centrifugal force will help partners to lift each other a bit.

Alabama Gal

Tennessee Folk Song
arranged by David J. Gonzol

* Text for use as a teaching aid.

2. I don't know how, how, *[3 times]*
   Alabama Gal.

3. I showed you how, how, *[3 times]*
   Alabama Gal.

4. Ain't I rock candy? *[3 times]*
   Alabama Gal.

LEAD THROUGH THAT SUGAR AND TEA

Concepts:

sol la   do re mi   sol

Teaching Suggestions:

- The teacher can model patching the drone as if with only Fs and Cs, next showing how to move the right hand for the D.
- The rhythm of the melody's first measure can be used to teach the woodblock part.
- The alto glockenspiel's pitches can be discovered by inverting the F and C of the drone, with the teacher modeling the rhythm.

Dance: Contra dance formation.

Verse 1: For the first phrase, the head couple joins hands and walks between the lines to the foot of the set. On the second phrase, they *right* swing each other, ending up facing the opposite partners of the foot couple.

Verse 2: The head couple each *left* swings the opposite partner at the foot. On the second phrase, the head couple takes its place at the foot, and all couples *right* swing.

Verse 3: The old head couple (now at the foot) may lead a promenade of all the couples by holding hands in skating position (right hands above, left hands below) and turning right (or left) to march to the head of the set, turning again to march back to the foot (also called *casting off*).

The song recommences with a new head couple.

1. Lead through that sugar and tea, oh,
   Lead through that candy.
   You lead through that sugar and tea,
   And I'll lead through that candy.

2. You swing that sugar and tea, oh,
   I'll swing that candy.
   We'll all swing that sugar and tea,
   And I'll swing that candy.

3. Promenade that sugar and tea, oh,
   Promenade that candy.
   You promenade that sugar and tea,
   And I'll promenade that candy.

Lead Through That Sugar and Tea

Oklahoma Folk Song
arranged by David J. Gonzol

Lead through that su-gar and tea, oh, lead through that can - dy.

You lead through that su-gar and tea, And I'll lead through that can - dy.

HERE WE GO ZOOTIE-O

Concepts:

sol la   do   mi

Teaching Suggestions:

- After students learn to sing the bass xylophone part with the suggested (temporary) text, they can try to find it on an instrument. They may discover that bass bars work well, or that the G can be played above the C rather than below. Orchestral instruments (e.g., string bass, trombone) make excellent substitutes, and may necessitate transposing to the key of B-flat.
- The teacher can model the alto xylophone part by singing it against the bass xylophone part. Again, students may find that other instruments (clarinets, French horns, etc.) work well, possibly adding the chord root (C).
- Rhythmic speech helps in teaching this classic cymbal ride—and other percussion parts might be invented to help the jazzy swing.
- The arrangement may be performed vocally, accompanied or unaccompanied.
- If desired, chromatic decorations may be used with the alto xylophone part, especially when substituting orchestral instruments:

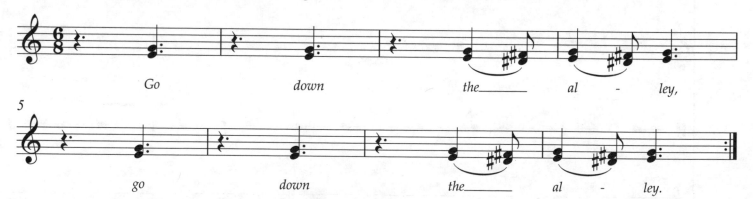

Go   down   the_____   al - ley,

go   down   the_____   al - ley.

Play Party:

Verse 1: Contra dance formation (two facing lines). Cross and hold hands with the partner across; alternate pulling of arms.

Verse 2: To form the alley, clap and jump back on the first few back beats.

Verse 3: Head couple comes down the alley to the foot, but *not* by walking, and never the same as anyone else. This Pennsylvania version of *Zootie-O* was played so people could display their finery, so be creative!

Repeat with new head couple.

Here We Go Zootie-O

Pennsylvania play party
arranged by David J. Gonzol

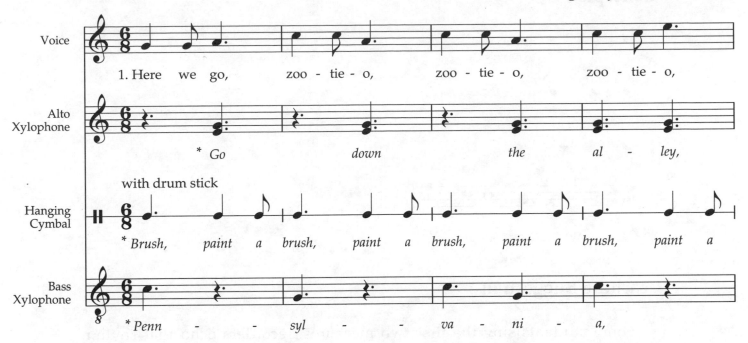

* Text for use as a teaching aid.

2. Step back Sally-o, Sally-o, Sally-o,
   Step back Sally-o, all night long.

3. Going through the alley-o, alley-o, alley-o,
   Going through the alley-o, all night long.

LI'L 'LIZA JANE

Concepts:

do re mi   sol la   do

Teaching Suggestions:

- Some students sing the first two measures, recorders echo that rhythm ♫ ♫ ♫ ♩ on an F, as a response. Then some students sing measures 1–2, 5–6, 9–10, and 13–14, with recorders always playing that response. Change the rhythm to ♫ ♫ ♩ ♩ and gradually introduce the actual pitches of the recorder part in measures 3–4, 7–8, 11–12, and 15–16. Lastly, add the F and C half notes tied to a quarter.
- If the bass xylophone plays all quarter notes at first, students can observe that the part needs more rhythmic interest. Change the second measure of the ostinato to the rhythm of "L'il Liza" (♪ ♩ ♪), then change the fourth measure to the rhythm of "go with me" (♫ ♩).
- The hand drum part is the "go with me" rhythm played backwards, followed by a quarter note and a quarter rest (♩ ♫ ♩ ♩ 𝄽).

Movement Suggestion:

With verses and a refrain, students can experiment with various traditional play party movements (sashaying, peeling the orange, reeling, etc.) for each section.

Li'l 'Liza Jane

arranged by David J. Gonzol

2. I've got a house in Baltimore, Li'l 'Liza Jane,
Street car runs right by my door, Li'l 'Liza Jane.
Refrain

3. I've got a house in Baltimore, Li'l 'Liza Jane,
Brussels carpet on the floor, Li'l 'Liza Jane.
Refrain

4. I've got a house in Baltimore, Li'l 'Liza Jane,
Silver doorplate on the door, Li'l Liza Jane.
Refrain

STOOPING ON THE WINDOW

Concepts:

la do re mi sol

Teaching Suggestions:

- Close ensemble can produce an appropriate rhythmic "groove." The accompaniment introduces figures found in some popular music. Patching the bass drum part in the left hand and the tambourine part in the right hand will clarify how they relate. If desired, speaking the rhythm syllables for these two parts (e.g., too too ta ta ta ta) can prepare students for using the same rhythm syllables to learn other parts. The bass drum and tambourine parts could be transferred to a bass and snare in a drum set.

- The rhythm of the bass xylophone/contrabass bar part can be learned through modeling. Discovering that the A-section is *do*-centered and the B-section is *la*-centered can lead students to play the correct pitches.

- Reading and singing solfège syllables can aid in learning the other parts (with E and B bars removed):

- If learned through solfège, instruments can be rearranged in G-*do* pentatonic, and the arrangement easily transposed, especially if that better accommodates the students' vocal range.
- Experiment using string bass (acoustic or electric) or additional percussion ostinati.
- Solos may be improvised over the accompaniment.

Games:

Game 1: Join hands in a line and slowly proceed in a tightening spiral, unwinding sharply after reaching the center. The leader may call, "Stooping on the window," with the others responding, "Wind the ball."

Game 2: Join hands in a line, with the leader holding a ball and the last two people holding their hands in an arch. The leader leads all through the arch, into a spiral, unwinding after reaching the center.

Stooping on the Window

arranged by David J. Gonzol

Stoop - ing   on   the   win - dow,   Wind   the   ball.___

Stoop - ing   on   the   win - dow,   Wind   the   ball.___

HANGING OUT THE LINEN CLOTHES

Concepts:

do   re   mi   fa

Teaching Suggestions:

- The melody is helpful for reinforcing *fa*.
- This is played additively: The bass metallophone (instrument 1) accompanies verse 1, the soprano metallophone joins in verse 2, etc. The first to sixth endings are a repeat of measures 7 and 8 and can be taught as such. They are designed to give time for pantomime changes between verses. If more time is needed, measures 5–8 may suffice.
- Parts may be taught in the order they are added.
- The bass and soprano metallophone parts constitute a level bordun.
- The bass and alto xylophone parts are arpeggiated borduns, ascending and descending respectively.
- The bongo and conga parts (or other suitably high and low drums) are easily read, but the guiro part must be taught with care. Lead the students to observe that it may be too dull playing only ‖: ♩ ‽ ᲃ ‽ ᲃ ♫ :‖ and that the sixteenth note figure enlivens it—yet this may make measures 9 and 10 tricky to play.
- The soprano and alto glockenspiel part should be familiar—after singing it (with the traditional text) students can discover how to play it.
- An introduction may be invented.

2. … Tuesday … , A-hanging out …

3. … Wednesday … , A-taking in …

4. … Thursday … , A-ironing …

$\quad\quad\quad\quad\quad\quad$ ♩ $\quad$ ♪

5. … Friday … , A-mend-ing …

6. … Saturday … , A-folding up …

$\quad\quad\quad\quad\quad\quad$ ♩ $\quad$ ♪

7. … Sunday … , A-wear-ing…

Hanging Out the Linen Clothes

American Folk Song
arranged by David J. Gonzol

FOLLOW THE DRINKING GOURD

Concepts:

syncopation
ties
incomplete natural minor:

mi   sol la ti do re mi

Students may pantomime the story while Jeanette Winter's evocative picture book is read aloud, singing the song each time it is mentioned. Costumes may be added, but need not be limited to people; animals, trees, and rivers can be represented by students as well. The escape route can meander across a room, with the Big Dipper on the north wall as the destination. The lengthy, dangerous process of escape, enduring hazards and savoring friendly assistance, can make the Underground Railroad come alive as students play the part of slaves who depend on a song for their very lives. Lessons about slavery are difficult because they are about people abusing people. Yet, sensitive teaching can show just how wrong such abuse is, and how people—and music—can provide hope in nearly impossible situations.

Teaching Suggestions:

- Patching the bass metallophone part by rote, one two-measure phrase at a time, teaches the phrase structure *a a b a*.
- Recorder students can read the A–C–D pattern once, then play that identical pattern as phrases 1, 2, and 4—resting throughout phrase 3. Then the notation in phrases 2 and 4 can be changed to include the quarter notes (adding the second A). Derive phrase 3 by playing A–C–D backwards.
- If desired, an instrument may double the melody—perhaps an alto or sopranino recorder, clarinet, or violin.
- Other incidental music may be created to accompany the story. Additional verses may be found in Winter's book.

Suggested Resources:

Bial, R. (1995). *The underground railroad.* Boston: Houghton Mifflin.

Gonzol, D. J. (1999, Spring). Follow the drinking gourd. *Minnesota Elementary Music Educators Notes, 21,* 14–15.

Gorrell, G. K. (1997). *North star to freedom: The story of the underground railroad.* New York: Delacorte.

Monjo, F. N., & Brenner, F. (Illustrator). (1970). *The drinking gourd: A story of the underground railroad.* New York: Harper.

Monjo, F. N., & Brenner, F. (Illustrator). (1997). *La Osa Menor: Una historia del Ferrocarril Subterraneo* (T. Mlawlor, Translator). New York: Harper.

Rall, G. D. (1994, September). Follow the drinking gourd. *The Planetarian, 23,* 8–12.

Ringgold, F. (1992). *Aunt Harriet's underground railroad in the sky.* New York: Crown.

Winter, J. (1988). *Follow the drinking gourd.* New York: Alfred A. Knopf.

Follow the Drinking Gourd

American Folk Song
arranged by David J. Gonzol

ROUND THE CORNER, SALLY

Concepts:

sol la   do re   sol

accompaniment: major, including *fa* and *ti*

This sea shanty, sung while pulling halyards (ropes to raise or lower sails), refers to rounding dangerous Cape Horn. So-called halyards such as this were often sung as call and response.

Teaching Suggestions:

- Model measures 1–2 and 5–6 of the bass xylophone part. Then add measures 3–4. Teach measures 7–8 as the inversion of measures 3–4.
- Similarly, model measures 1–2 and 5–6 of the soprano recorder part. After adding measures 3–4, teach measures 7–8 as part of a sequence pattern, beginning on B (as in mm. 3–4), then A, etc.
- Measures 1–2 and 5–6 of the alto xylophone part may be tried as quarter notes on beats one and two, all Ds and Gs. When students notice the dissonance in measure 2, the D can be changed to an E (with the bass xylophone's C, implying the subdominant chord, *fa–la–do*). Gs in measure 4 will create dissonance, so they may be changed to F-sharps (the dominant chord, *sol-ti-re*). Use a similar process for measures 7–8, finally changing the rhythm to rests and eighth notes as written.
- The rhythm of the melody in measure 2 becomes the alto glockenspiel "color" part (♫♩ ♩).
- Reversed, that rhythm becomes the hand drum ostinato (‖: ♩ ♫♩ :‖).
- Because the tambourine part is derived from the melody's sixteenth notes, it can be taught with speech: e.g., "Way, [rest, rest] corner and away."
- Extemporizing shanty verses is very authentic. In that spirit, although a halyard is not a play-party, the verses might suggest the creation of play-party-like movement.

1.   *Call:* Round the corner and away we go,
   Response: Round the corner, Sally,
       Call: Round the corner and away we go,
   Response: Round the corner, Sally.

2.   *Call:* Thought I heard the old man say,
   Response: Round the corner, Sally,
       Call: One more pull and then belay,
   Response: Round the corner, Sally.

3.   *Call:* One more pull and that will do,
   Response: Round the corner, Sally,
       Call: We're the boys to kick 'er through,
   Response: Round the corner, Sally.

Round the Corner, Sally

arranged by David J. Gonzol

Round the cor-ner and a - way we go, round the cor-ner, Sal - ly.

Round the cor-ner and a - way we go, Round the cor - ner, Sal - ly.

WHO KILLED COCK ROBIN?

Concepts:

la   do re mi   la

accompaniment: *la* natural minor, including *fa* and *ti*

recorder skill:

Opportunities for solos and drama are given with this song. Margaret Wise Brown's sensitive story, *The Dead Bird*, illustrates what many of us have done with animals we found. Accordingly, experiment with sensitive orchestrations—perhaps using the bass xylophone and contrabass bar (E) throughout, dedicating the alto glockenspiel for the fly's verse, the snare drum for the snipe's, etc. In combining parts, take care so that voices remain balanced.

Teaching Suggestions:

- If the students are told that *mi* is the first pitch, they may determine that the first phrase (measures 1–2) is built on a fifth (*la-mi*) usable as an E and B drone. They may discover that in the second phrase an A is prominent, and that B's neighbors, A and C, can be used in the bass xylophone part at that point.
- While the alto glockenspiel part is easily taught as a type of inversion of the drone, its first measure of rhythm can be used to teach the bass drum part, which alternates the rhythm to complement the alto glockenspiel part.
- The snare drum part can be taught via a process as follows:

1. Play 4 times:

2. Add the sixteenths and play 4 times:

3. Add the first beat's eighth notes in measures 1 and 5, playing measures 1–8:

- In examining the melody, students can see that sixteenth notes animate its second half, while measures 2, 4, and 8 have the least rhythmic complexity.
- For the recorder part, put sixteenths and a quarter note in measures 2, 4, and 8, resting in the other measures. Then, fill in the other measures with the notes of less motion.

26

- Use the alto glockenspiel part's first measure for the second measure of the descant—but reverse the beats' order. The only note not yet used in any part, D, can be used in constructing the remainder of the descant.
- Entrances of parts may be layered, in various combinations, over the verses. Perhaps begin with voice, bass metallophone and contrabass bar. Perhaps, too, on some verses, recorders can improvise in pentatonic.

Brown, M. W., & Charlip, R. (Illustrator). (1958). *The dead bird*. New York: W. R. Scott.

Who Killed Cock Robin?

2. Who saw him die?
   "I," said the fly,
   "with my little teeney eye,"

   Refrain

3. Who caught his blood?
   "I," said the fish,
   "with my little silver dish,"

   Refrain

4. Who made his coffin?
   "I," said the snipe,
   "with my little pocket knife,"

   Refrain

5. Who made his shroud-en?
   "I," said the beetle,
   "with my little sewing needle,"

   Refrain

6. Who dug his grave?
   "I," said the crow,
   "with my little spade and hoe,"

   Refrain

7. Who hauled him to it?
   "I," said the bear,
   "just as hard as I could tear,"

   Refrain

8. Who let him down?
   "I," said the crane,
   "with my little golden chain,"

   Refrain

9. Who pat his grave?
   "I," said the duck,
   "with my big old splatter foot,"

   Refrain

10. Who preached his funeral?
    "I," said the lark,
    "with a song and a harp,"

    Refrain

DOWN IN THAT VALLEY

Concepts:

♩

𝅝

Phrygian mode

recorder skill:

Teaching Suggestions:

- Determine the solfège syllables for the last three measures of the melody to discover that the Phrygian mode can be sung as a scale based on *mi*.
- Further discover that a fifth above *mi* yields a drone on *mi* and *ti* (in this case, E and B).
- Hear that the B clashes somewhat with the melody in the third measure of each phrase. Experiment changing to a neighboring A or C in measures 3 and 7. As both A and C are harmonically appropriate, assign the A to the bass xylophone and the C to the soprano metallophone.
- Add the alto metallophone on beat two of each measure.
- Use the basic drone pitches E and B to teach the soprano and alto glockenspiel parts; add the G and passing tone A in the second phrase.
- Take the rhythm of the glockenspiel part in measure five (♩   ♩ ♩) and play it backwards, then transfer it to an E on the soprano recorder. Add a whole note, and lastly change to the F upper neighbor tone. The E–F recorder skill can be practiced through echo and improvisation.
- Solo instruments may improvise for a verse or so; the metallophone trio alone might accompany effectively.
- For recorder improvisation, play only the alto and bass metallophone parts as written, but let the soprano metallophone player temporarily switch to playing his or her part on the alto metallophone.

No traditional movement is known for this sweetly melancholic song, yet creative movement can complement it.

Down in That Valley

Kentucky Folk Song
arranged by David J. Gonzol

CEDAR SWAMP

Concepts:

diminution
Mixolydian mode transposed to F

Teaching Suggestions:

- This mixolydian melody (the F may be sung as *sol*) should be performed with vigor.
- After teaching the verse's bass xylophone part using notation, one can ask what note is next in shortness to the quarter note, changing the two quarters to eighths. Similarly, the half note is changed to a quarter, and this version in diminution played for the refrain.
- The tambourine part can be taught in a similar manner.
- Rhythmic speech can help teach the soprano xylophone and glockenspiel parts, deriving them from patterns in the melody.
- The alto xylophone part may be learned using this process, beginning with the left hand:

Step 1.
Play 4 times

Step 2.
Play 2 times

Step 3. With the right hand, add the G in measure 4.

Step 4. One by one, each C (all right hand) can be added, perhaps beginning with measure 2 or 4, for example:

- The following rhythmic speech may be used to learn the soprano xylophone part:

Swamp,   yon-der in the

- Strive for authentic country portamentos in measures 4 and 10, experiment with thinner textures in some verses—and swing with joy!

Dance:

For this play party in contra dance formation, the head couple sashays down and back on the verses, and reels to the foot on the refrain, as in *Alabama Gal*.

Cedar Swamp

Kentucky Folk Song
arranged by David J. Gonzol

2. Black-eyed girl is mad at me,
   Blue-eyed girl won't have me.
   'Fore I marry the cross-eyed girl,
   A single life I'll tarry.

   Refrain

3. Built my love a fine brick house,
   Built it in the garden;
   Put her in but she hopped out,
   So fare you well, my darlin'.

   Refrain

4. The older she gets the prettier she gets,
   I tell you, she's a honey.
   She makes me work all through the week
   And get stove wood on Sunday.

   Refrain